3 9077 08209 4163

S0-BNT-302

SOCIAL PROGRESS AND SUSTAINABILITY

Shelter • Safety • Literacy • Health • Freedom • Environment

NORTH AMERICA

Foreword by **Michael Green,**
Executive Director, Social Progress Imperative

By Judy Boyd

SOCIAL PROGRESS AND SUSTAINABILITY

SOCIAL PROGRESS AND SUSTAINABILITY

Shelter • Safety • Literacy • Health • Freedom • Environment

NORTH AMERICA

Judy Boyd

Foreword by
Michael Green
Executive Director, Social Progress Imperative

MASON CREST
MASON CREST PUBLISHERS
Broomall, PA

Mason Crest Publishers Inc.
450 Parkway Drive, Suite D
Broomall, PA 19008
www.masoncrest.com

Printed in the United States of America

First printing
9 8 7 6 5 4 3 2 1

Series ISBN: 978-1-4222-3490-7
Hardcover ISBN: 978-1-4222-3498-3
ebook ISBN: 978-1-4222-8393-6

Library of Congress Cataloging-in-Publication Data

Names: Boyd, Judy, 1950– author.
Title: North America/by Judy Boyd; foreword by Michael Green, executive director, Social Progress Imperative.
Description: Broomall, PA : Mason Crest, 2017. | Series: Social progress and sustainability | Includes index.
Identifiers: LCCN 2016007609| ISBN 9781422234983 (hardback) | ISBN 9781422234907 (series) | ISBN 9781422283936 (ebook)
Subjects: LCSH: Social indicators—North America—Juvenile literature. | North America—Social conditions—Juvenile literature. | North America—Economic conditions—Juvenile literature.
Classification: LCC HN50 .B69 2017 | DDC 306.097—dc23
LC record available at http://lccn.loc.gov/2016007609
Developed and Produced by Print Matters Productions, Inc. (www.printmattersinc.com)

Project Editor: David Andrews
Design: Bill Madrid, Madrid Design
Copy Editor: Laura Daly

CONTENTS

KEY ICONS TO LOOK FOR:

 Text-Dependent Questions: These questions send the reader back to the text for more careful attention to the evidence presented there.

 Words to Understand: These words with their easy-to-understand definitions will increase the reader's understanding of the text, while building vocabulary skills.

 Series Glossary of Key Terms: This back-of-the book glossary contains terminology used throughout this series. Words found here increase the reader's ability to read and comprehend higher-level books and articles in this field.

 Research Projects: Readers are pointed toward areas of further inquiry connected to each chapter. Suggestions are provided for projects that encourage deeper research and analysis.

 Sidebars: This boxed material within the main text allows readers to build knowledge, gain insights, explore possibilities, and broaden their perspectives by weaving together additional information to provide realistic and holistic perspectives.

SOCIAL PROGRESS AROUND THE GLOBE

Michael Green

How do you measure the success of a country? It's not as easy as you might think.

Americans are used to thinking of their country as the best in the world, but what does "best" actually mean? For a long time, the United States performed better than any other country in terms of the sheer size of its economy, and bigger was considered better. Yet China caught up with the United States in 2014 and now has a larger overall economy.

What about average wealth? The United States does far better than China here but not as well as several countries in Europe and the Middle East.

Most of us would like to be richer, but is money really what we care about? Is wealth really how we want to measure the success of countries—or cities, neighborhoods, families, and individuals? Would you really want to be rich if it meant not having access to the World Wide Web, or suffering a painful disease, or not being safe when you walked near your home?

Using money to compare societies has a long history, including the invention in the 1930s of an economic measurement called gross domestic product (GDP). Basically, GDP for the United States "measures the output of goods and services produced by labor and property located within the U.S. during a given time period." The concept of GDP was actually created by the economist Simon Kuznets for use by the federal government. Using measures like GDP to guide national economic policies helped pull the United States out of the Great Depression and helped Europe and Japan recover after World War II. As they say in business school, if you can measure it, you can manage it.

Many positive activities contribute to GDP, such as

- Building schools and roads
- Growing crops and raising livestock
- Providing medical care

More and more experts, however, are seeing that we may need another way to measure the success of a nation.

Other kinds of activities increase a country's GDP, but are these signs that a country is moving in a positive direction?

- Building and maintaining larger prisons for more inmates
- Cleaning up after hurricanes or other natural disasters
- Buying alcohol and illegal drugs
- Maintaining ecologically unsustainable use of water, harvesting of trees, or catching of fish

GDP also does not address inequality. A few people could become extraordinarily wealthy, while the rest of a country is plunged into poverty and hunger, but this wouldn't be reflected in the GDP.

In the turbulent 1960s, Robert F. Kennedy, the attorney general of the United States and brother of President John F. Kennedy, famously said of GDP during a 1968 address to students at the University of Kansas: "It counts napalm and counts nuclear warheads and armored cars for the police to fight the riots in our cities ... [but] the gross national product does not allow for the health of our children.... [I]t measures everything in short, except that which makes life worthwhile."

For countries like the United States that already have large or strong economies, it is not clear that simply making the economy larger will improve human welfare. Developed countries struggle with issues like obesity, diabetes, crime, and environmental challenges. Increasingly, even poorer countries are struggling with these same issues.

Noting the difficulties that many countries experience as they grow wealthier (such as increased crime and obesity), people around the world have begun to wonder: What if we measure the things we really care about directly, rather than assuming that greater GDP will mean improvement in everything we care about? Is that even possible?

The good news is that it is. There is a new way to think about prosperity, one that does not depend on measuring economic activity using traditional tools like GDP.

Advocates of the "Beyond GDP" movement, people ranging from university professors to leaders of businesses, from politicians to religious leaders, are calling for more attention to directly measuring things we all care about, such as hunger, homelessness, disease, and unsafe water.

One of the new tools that has been developed is called the Social Progress Index (SPI), and it is the data from this index that is featured in this series of books, Social Progress and Sustainability.

The SPI has been created to measure and advance social progress outcomes at a fine level of detail in communities of different sizes and at different levels of wealth. This means that we can compare the performance of very different countries using one standard set of measurements, to get a sense of how well different countries perform compared to each other. The index measures how the different parts of society, including governments, businesses, not-for-profits, social entrepreneurs, universities, and colleges, work together to improve human welfare. Similarly, it does not strictly measure the actions taken in a particular place. Instead, it measures the outcomes in a place.

The SPI begins by defining what it means to be a good society, structured around three fundamental themes:

- Do people have the basic needs for survival: food, water, shelter, and safety?
- Do people have the building blocks of a better future: education, information, health, and sustainable ecosystems?

- Do people have a chance to fulfill their dreams and aspirations by having rights and freedom of choice, without discrimination, with access to the cutting edge of human knowledge?

The Social Progress Index is published each year, using the best available data for all the countries covered. You can explore the data on our website at http://socialprogressimperative.org. The data for this series of books is from our 2015 index, which covered 133 countries. Countries that do not appear in the 2015 index did not have the right data available to be included.

A few examples will help illustrate how overall Social Progress Index scores compare to measures of economic productivity (for example, GDP per capita), and also how countries can differ on specific lenses of social performance.

- The United States (6th for GDP per capita, 16th for SPI overall) ranks 6th for Shelter but 68th in Health and Wellness, because of factors such as obesity and death from heart disease.
- South Africa (62nd for GDP per capita, 63rd for SPI) ranks 44th in Access to Information and Communications but only 114th in Health and Wellness, because of factors such as relatively short life expectancy and obesity.
- India (93rd for GDP per capita, 101st for SPI) ranks 70th in Personal Rights but only 128th in Tolerance and Inclusion, because of factors such as low tolerance for different religions and low tolerance for homosexuals.
- China (66th for GDP per capita, 92nd for SPI) ranks 58th in Shelter but 84th in Water and Sanitation, because of factors such as access to piped water.
- Brazil (55th for GDP per capita, 42nd for SPI) ranks 61st in Nutrition and Basic Medical Care but only 122nd in Personal Safety, because of factors such as a high homicide rate.

The Social Progress Index focuses on outcomes. Politicians can boast that the government has spent millions on feeding the hungry; the SPI measures how well fed people really are. Businesses can boast investing money in their operations or how many hours their employees have volunteered in the community; the SPI measures actual literacy rates and access to the Internet. Legislators and administrators might focus on how much a country spends on health care; the SPI measures how long and how healthily people live. The index doesn't measure whether countries have passed laws against discrimination; it measures whether people experience discrimination. And so on.

- What if your family measured its success only by the amount of money it brought in but ignored the health and education of members of the family?
- What if a neighborhood focused only on the happiness of the majority while discriminating against one family because they were different?
- What if a country focused on building fast cars but was unable to provide clean water and air?

The Social Progress Index can also be adapted to measure human well-being in areas smaller than a whole country.

- A Social Progress Index for the Amazon region of Brazil, home to 24 million people and covering one of the world's most precious environmental assets, shows how 800 different municipalities compare. A map of that region shows where needs are greatest and is informing a development strategy for the region that balances the interests of people and the planet. Nonprofits, businesses, and governments in Brazil are now using this data to improve the lives of the people living in the Amazon region.
- The European Commission—the governmental body that manages the European Union—is using the Social Progress Index to compare the performance of multiple regions in each of 28 countries and to inform development strategies.
- We envision a future where the Social Progress Index will be used by communities of different sizes around the world to measure how well they are performing and to help guide governments, businesses, and nonprofits to make better choices about what they focus on improving, including learning lessons from other communities of similar size and wealth that may be performing better on some fronts. Even in the United States subnational social progress indexes are underway to help direct equitable growth for communities.

The Social Progress Index is intended to be used along with economic measurements such as GDP, which have been effective in guiding decisions that have lifted hundreds of millions of people out of abject poverty. But it is designed to let countries go even further, not just making economies larger but helping them devote resources to where they will improve social progress the most. The vision of my organization, the Social Progress Imperative, which created the Social Progress Index, is that in the future the Social Progress Index will be considered alongside GDP when people make decisions about how to invest money and time.

Imagine if we could measure what charities and volunteers really contribute to our societies. Imagine if businesses competed based on their whole contribution to society—not just economic, but social and environmental. Imagine if our politicians were held accountable for how much they made people's lives better, in real, tangible ways. Imagine if everyone, everywhere, woke up thinking about how their community performed on social progress and about what they could do to make it better.

Note on Text:

While Michael Green wrote the foreword and data is from the 2015 Social Progress Index, the rest of the text is not by Michael Green or the Social Progress Imperative.

This political map shows the countries of the region discussed in this book.

SOCIAL PROGRESS IN NORTH AMERICA

North America is a vast region that stretches from the steamy jungles of the tropics to the permafrost wilderness of the Arctic Circle. This book explores the level of social progress in the three countries of North America: Canada, the United States, and Mexico. Social progress is a society's ability to meet the basic human needs of its citizens, create the building blocks that individuals and communities use to improve the quality of their lives, and make it possible for everyone to reach their potential. The book examines bare necessities, such as people's access to food, water, shelter, and basic medical care; it also considers whether people are safe, receive education, and enjoy personal freedom. It considers as well the political and natural environment.

To understand how social progress differs from one country to another, the Social Progress Imperative scored 133 countries around the world in three main areas:

Basic Human Needs: *Does a country provide for its people's most essential needs?*

Foundations of Well-being: *Are the building blocks in place for individuals and communities to enhance and sustain well-being?*

Opportunity: *Is there opportunity for all individuals to reach their full potential?*

After scores were calculated, the countries were ranked from the highest score (best) to the lowest score (worst) and placed in one of six groups ranging from Very High Social Progress to Very Low Social Progress. The table below shows the SPI scores, rankings, and progress grouping for the North American countries.

	CANADA Very High Social Progress		UNITED STATES High Social Progress		MEXICO Upper Middle Social Progress	
	Score	Rank	Score	Rank	Score	Rank
Basic Human Needs	94.89	7th	91.23	21st	71.81	73rd
Foundation of Well-being	79.22	14th	75.15	35th	68.82	71st
Opportunity	86.58	1st	82.18	8th	60.88	40th
Overall Social Progress Score	86.89	6th	82.85	16th	67.50	54th

Source: Social Progress Index

Red numbers highlight where a country's score is relatively weak compared to other countries with economies of a similar size. Blue numbers show a relative strength, and black numbers show where each country performs about the same as countries with similar wealth.

The chapters that follow explore some of the stories behind the scores and look at some of the reasons for relative strengths and weaknesses. You'll see how wealth and social progress are not always related and how a high score does not mean that high social progress applies to everyone.

US President Barack Obama, his Mexican counterpart, Enrique Peña Nieto, and Canadian Prime Minister Stephen Harper walk together during the North America Leaders' Summit in Toluca, Mexico.

Volunteers serve at a soup kitchen.

CHAPTER 1

BASIC HUMAN NEEDS

Words to Understand

Child mortality rate: the number of children that die before their fifth birthday for every 1,000 babies born alive.

Communicable diseases: diseases transmitted from one person or animal to another. Also called contagious or infectious diseases.

Drug cartel: a criminal group in the business of transporting and selling illegal drugs.

Food desert: a neighborhood or community with no walking access to affordable, nutritious food.

Food security: having reliable access to sufficient, safe, nutritious food.

Income inequality: when the wealth of a country is spread very unevenly among the population.

Maternal mortality rate: the number of pregnant women who die for every 100,000 births.

The first thing to look at when judging a country's social progress is how well the basic human needs of its citizens are being met. Basic human needs are the things people need to keep them alive: enough food, clean water, improved sanitation, adequate shelter, and access to basic medical care. People also need to be safe and to feel safe. If your neighborhood is controlled by criminals, if your country is at war, if you are homeless or have a violent home life, your basic human needs aren't being met. To compare how well countries around the world take care of the basic needs of their people, the Social Progress Imperative looked at 133 countries and scored them in four categories:

1. Water and Sanitation: *Can people drink the water without getting sick?*
2. Nutrition and Basic Medical Care: *Do people have enough to eat? Can they see a doctor?*
3. Shelter: *Do people have housing with basic utilities, such as electricity?*
4. Personal Safety: *Are people safe from violence? Do they feel afraid?*

This table shows the SPI scores and world rankings among the 133 SPI countries for Canada, the United States, and Mexico:

	CANADA		UNITED STATES		MEXICO	
	Score	Rank	Score	Rank	Score	Rank
GDP per capita	$41,894	14th	$51,340	6th	$16,291	51st
Water and sanitation	99.23	24th	98.68	28th	88.47	56th
Nutrition and medical care	99.05	28th	98.52	39th	96.27	62nd
Shelter	89.61	7th	90.05	6th	71.48	55th
Personal safety	91.66	8th	77.66	30th	35.03	124th
Overall Basic Human Needs	94.89	7th	91.23	21st	72.81	73rd

Wealthy countries like the United States and Canada do a good job of meeting the basic needs of most of their citizens. It makes sense that they score higher than Mexico, which has far less money to spend on public projects and programs.

The red numbers in the table tell an interesting story. They highlight scores that are lower than the scores of other countries around the world with a similar gross domestic product (GDP) per capita (per person). For example, even though the United States has the 6th-largest economy in the world, it scores lower in almost every category than Canada, whose economy ranks 14th. Clearly, social progress does not depend entirely on money.

U.S. household spending

The working poor spend a larger share of their income on food, housing and health care than do more affluent Americans. Average spending by category, 2012:

	$15,000- 20,000	$50,000- 75,000	More than $150,000
Food	15.4%	13.0%	10.4%
Housing	39.4	32.6	29.3
Transportation	16.1	19.9	14.9
Health care	8.5	7.4	5.1
Insurance, retirement	3.2	9.8	17.7
Entertainment	4.4	5.1	6.0
Education	1.6	1.3	4.4
Apparel, personal care	4.8	4.3	4.4
Miscellaneous	6.7	6.6	7.9

Source: U.S. Bureau of Labor Statistics
Graphic: The Commercial Appeal (Memphis, Tenn.)   © 2014 MCT

Table showing U.S. household spending by income group

Income inequality plays a role in lower scores, too, even in rich countries. **Income inequality** is when the wealth of a country is spread very unevenly among the population. Oxfam (oxfam.org), a charity that fights poverty, estimates that by 2016 the richest 1 percent of the world's population will have more wealth than the other 99 percent *combined.*

Water and Sanitation

Imagine that there is no toilet in your house. Flies and mosquitoes breed in sewage and open water tanks in your neighborhood. They spread deadly diseases, including diarrhea, cholera, typhoid, hepatitis, dengue fever, polio, and malaria. Many people in your community are sick but cannot afford a doctor. Children often die before their fifth birthday. This is reality for those without access to improved water and sanitation facilities.

In Mexico 3 of every 20 people are without improved water and sanitation. Water from wells can become contaminated with human waste, dangerous industrial chemicals, or pesticides and fertilizers from farms. Even tap water is often not safe to drink because dirty pipes and storage tanks can put harmful bacteria and lead in the water. Buying or gathering fuel to boil water is a financial burden on the poor.

A lot of Canadians and Americans would be surprised to learn that some of their fellow citizens have neither tap water they can drink nor modern sanitation facilities. Although it's a small percentage of the total population, there are still many people in rural areas of both countries who still lack these basic services.

When bottled water is the only option, it can cost as much as 10 percent of a poor person's income.

In North America the poor, minorities, indigenous groups, and immigrants are the most likely to be without clean water and sanitation. While most live in rural areas, they are also crowded into the city slums without these services. There are many reasons why water and sanitation projects don't reach everyone, including

- *Cost:* Water and sanitation projects require costly engineers and technology.
- *Lack of local expertise:* Most people are not trained to use and care for these complex systems.
- *Environmental injustice:* Rural areas get more than their share of polluting projects, such as landfills, mines, dirty industries, and animal operations.
- *Social injustice:* People without services are usually poor and belong to a minority group that is routinely denied service.

Those who live with the ill effects of dirty water and poor sanitation often suffer from poor nutrition and lack basic medical care.

Nutrition and Basic Medical Care

The World Food Summit of 1996 defined **food security** as "when all people at all times have access to sufficient, safe, nutritious *food* to maintain a healthy and active life." To have enough food, a region must be able to grow or import it for every person and deliver it to every community.

Fewer than 5 percent of North Americans don't get enough to eat; however, even this small percentage means that millions of people don't have enough food. The problem is worse in Mexico, where more than 50 percent of the people are undernourished.

Food Deserts

Even in countries with enough food, not every person eats well. The unemployed and the underemployed don't have enough money to buy all the food they need. Many people live in what are called food deserts. Food deserts are neighborhoods and communities with no walking access to affordable, nutritious food. Without a car, people living in food deserts depend on convenience stores and fast-food restaurants for meals. Their diet is mostly high-fat, high-sugar, processed foods with few whole grains or fresh vegetables, which can cause health problems like diabetes.

If this is your grocery store, what's for dinner?

One way to see whether people have access to basic medical care is to look at a country's **maternal mortality rate**, **child mortality rate**, and number of deaths from **communicable** (or infectious) **diseases** for every 100,000 people. The following table shows the SPI scores and world ranks for these categories for North America.

	CANADA		UNITED STATES		MEXICO	
	Score	Rank	Score	Rank	Score	Rank
Maternal mortality rate	11.0	33rd	28.0	55th	49.0	67th
Child mortality rate	5.2	29th	6.9	38th	14.5	59th
Deaths from communicable diseases	23.0	23rd	31.0	37th	57.0	58th

Again, the numbers in red highlight where the United States doesn't score as well as other high-income countries.

Shelter

Shelter is another basic human need. Shelter means a permanent structure with clean water, sanitation, and a reliable source of electricity. Homelessness is a problem for many in North America. People often become homeless because of events over which they have no control, for example, because of an increase in the price of food, the loss of a job, or getting sick.

Poverty, cuts to social welfare systems, low wages, and a lack of facilities for housing the mentally ill are major causes of homelessness in North America. A shortage of low-income housing is one of the main causes in Canada. The United States has more affordable and low-income housing than Canada and ranks higher in this category than other countries with similar economies.

We often think about homeless people as being alone, but this is not always the case. In the United States, for example, about half of the up to 3.5 million homeless people are families with children. In Canada one of every five homeless people is between 16 and 24 years old.

Source: Raising the Roof

Public awareness sign in a Canadian transit station.

How Do You End Homelessness?
Give People Homes

For many, the experience of homelessness is short because they get help from family members or through social services programs. Other people are what are called chronically homeless. These are people who have been homeless for more than one year or homeless four times in the past three years. According to the US Interagency Council on Homelessness (USICH), it costs between $30,000 and $50,000 per year to provide the chronically homeless with crisis services, including emergency rooms, jails, psychiatric facilities, and temporary shelters.

The big problem is that spending all that money on crisis services doesn't get homeless people off the street. In 2005, for example, the state of Utah developed a unique plan to end chronic homelessness: it started giving homes to homeless people. After 10 years, the plan reduced the number of chronically homeless people to fewer than 200 and saved the taxpayers a lot of money.

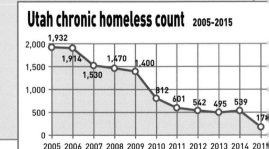

Utah chronic homeless count 2005-2015

Almost 50 percent of Mexico's citizens live in poverty, so many parents find that they cannot afford to feed their families. Sometimes they send their children to beg or sell things in the streets. Sometimes they abandon them there. As a result, millions of Mexican children live and work unsupervised on the streets of major cities. These street children struggle to stay alive and are at high risk for violence, kidnapping, and abuse by criminals and the police.

Personal Safety

Personal safety is about actually being safe and also about feeling safe. One way to measure personal safety is to look at crime statistics. Public agencies keep a record of crimes, accidents, injuries, and causes of deaths, among other things, that can be used to compare one country to another. Another way to measure personal safety is to simply ask people whether or not they feel safe where they live. This kind of answer can be measured by assigning a number from 1 to 5, where 1 = strongly no (I don't feel safe) and 5 = strongly yes (I do feel safe). When you add up the numbers from questions like this, you can compare the scores of one group to another group. The Social Progress Imperative included both kinds of measurements of personal safety to calculate the personal safety scores and world rankings for North American countries shown in the following chart.

	CANADA		UNITED STATES		MEXICO	
	Score	Rank	Score	Rank	Score	Rank
Personal safety	91.66	8th	77.66	30th	35.03	124th

Canada ranks very high and compares well to other countries in its economic class. The red numbers tell a different story for the United States and Mexico. Of the 133 countries included on the SPI, Mexico ranks near the bottom of the list for personal safety, at 124th. The United States ranks 30th, which is low for one of the world's wealthiest countries.

The low scores in the United States are related to the number of traffic deaths (ranks 38th), the number of homicides (ranks 41st), and the number of people in jail (more than any other developed country in the world). Even though the number of violent crimes in the United States has gone down in recent decades, the homicide rate remains higher than in other countries with similar economies. Some believe this is because the United States has more guns per person than any other country in the world (88 guns for every 100 people compared to 30 in Canada and 15 in Mexico). Others say that even though the number of deaths from firearms is higher in the United States, it's relatively low compared to the large number of guns in the country.

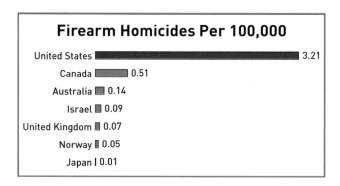

Firearm Homicides Per 100,000

United States — 3.21
Canada — 0.51
Australia — 0.14
Israel — 0.09
United Kingdom — 0.07
Norway — 0.05
Japan — 0.01

Mexico ranks low in several personal safety categories:

Homicide rate (ranks 113th)

Violent crime (ranks 124th)

Political terror: *Civil and political rights violations* (ranks 119th)

Perceived criminality: *Are fellow citizens trustworthy?* (ranks 94th)

Violence in Mexico is caused by a combination of widespread poverty and its ideal location for supplying illegal drugs to the United States. Americans spend about $100 billion every year on illegal drugs, most of which come into the country across the US–Mexico border. In 1972 US President Richard Nixon declared a "war on drugs." Since then, the United States has spent $1 trillion on both sides of the border in unsuccessful attempts to stop the flow of drugs from Mexico. The Mexican government has also dedicated a lot of money and resources to this task, with lost lives estimated to be in the tens of thousands.

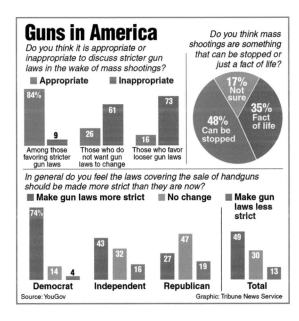

A poll on mass shootings and stricter gun laws in the United States.

Criminal business groups called **drug cartels** control the flow of drugs through Mexico and have connections to criminal gangs in many US cities. Cartels use bribes and ruthless violence, including torture and beheading, against those who try to stop them. Because the drug business is so profitable (over $60 billion per year), the cartels have more money than the Mexican government to buy assault weapons (usually from the United States) and to pay and train its "soldiers." The leaders of Mexico's drug cartels are some of the richest people in the world. Joaquin "El Chapo" Guzman, once head of the powerful Sinaloa Cartel, was named the 10th-richest man in Mexico in 2011. Cartels take in billions of dollars a year and are able to offer generous bribes to government officials and law enforcement to ignore their criminal activities.

While most people agree that the drug war has been a costly failure, there is little agreement as to how to fix it. It's clear that reducing poverty in Mexico and investing in drug education and prevention programs in the United States would help. In recent years, many in the United States have supported legalizing recreational drugs such as marijuana and decriminalizing drug use, so that otherwise law-abiding users would not end up in jail.

How Can You Help?

Many local organizations work to end poverty in North America. Some welcome young volunteers to help with activities like food, book, and clothing drives. You can search online to find volunteer opportunities in your area. Here are a few links to get you started:

Habitat for Humanity Youth Programs (United States/Canada)

habitat.org/youthprograms

American Red Cross

www.redcross.org/support/volunteer/young-humanitarians

Do Something

www.dosomething.org/volunteer/poverty

 ## Text-Dependent Questions

1. Which people in North America are most likely to be without clean water and sanitation?
2. Which North American country shows a relative weakness in its maternal and child mortality rates?
3. What percentage of people in Mexico don't get enough to eat?
3. In which North American country are you least likely to die from a communicable disease?
4. Name two advantages of giving homes to chronically homeless people.
5. Give three reasons for Mexico's low overall score in the Personal Safety category.

Research Project

View a map of food deserts in the United States. Find out whether your area qualifies as a food desert. If it does, it may qualify for government funding for healthy retail food outlets.

1. Go to ers.usda.gov/data-products/food-access-research-atlas.aspx on the website of the United States Department of Agriculture. Read all the information on that page.

2. Click on ENTER THE MAP. Enter a place name or zip code of a place that interests you.

3. When you finish looking at addresses, zoom out on the map to get a state or national view. Experiment with displaying the four data layers one at a time and in various combinations. Turn layers on and off using the check boxes next to their descriptions.
   The Low Income (LI) and Low Access (LA) layers show areas that have low income data with low access data of different distances. The LI and LA at 1 and 10 miles layer, for example, highlights those areas with both low income *and* low access to nutritious food measured at 1 mile and at 10 miles. This is the original definition of a food desert.

4. Click on ▶ Component Layers. Experiment with turning these layers on and off one at a time and in combinations. Do you see any patterns that surprise you? Are the low-income areas where you thought they would be? Why are there such large areas of low vehicle access in the West? Why are these areas smaller in the East? Come up with other questions that you can answer with the map.

The true measure of a nation's prosperity is how well it meets the needs of its least-advantaged people.

A student and teacher in Calgary Canada, discuss work in a classroom

CHAPTER 2

FOUNDATIONS OF WELL-BEING

Words to Understand

Adult literacy rate: the percentage of adults age 15 or older who can read and write.

Deforestation: the cutting down or clearing of trees with no intention of replanting.

Greenhouse gas emissions: the release of gases, especially carbon dioxide, into the earth's atmosphere absorb infrared radiation from the sun and generate heat. More gases generate more heat and the earth's atmosphere gets warmer. This warming of the atmosphere is known as the "greenhouse effect."

Groundwater: water that is stored naturally underground.

Primary education: basic education for children (usually ages 5 to 11), including reading, writing, and basic math. For most countries, primary education is mandatory. Also called elementary education.

Secondary education: generally, education past the primary level. In developed countries, it is usually mandatory.

To see how well 133 countries are doing at offering the building blocks that citizens and communities use to create better lives, the Social Progress Imperative looked at four areas:

- **Access to basic knowledge:** *Can children go to school? Can adults read and write?*
- **Access to information and communication:** *Do people have Internet? Mobile (or cell) phones? Are they free to disagree with those in power?*

- **Health and wellness:** *How long do people live? Do they die early from treatable diseases?*
- **Ecosystem sustainability:** *Will future generations have a healthy environment in which to live?*

Here are the SPI scores and rankings for Canada, the United States, and Mexico in each category:

	CANADA		UNITED STATES		MEXICO	
	Score	Rank	Score	Rank	Score	Rank
GDP per capita	$41,894	14th	$51,340	6th	$16,291	51st
Access to basic knowledge	98.17	18th	95.33	45th	92.46	64th
Access to information and communications	84.56	25th	85.00	23rd	62.30	91st
Health and wellness	76.09	17th	68.66	68th	72.02	45th
Ecosystem sustainability	58.04	48th	51.63	74th	48.50	90th
Overall Foundations of Well-being	79.22	14th	75.15	35th	68.82	71st

A quick look at the table shows that Canada scores a lot higher than Mexico in the category of Access to Information and Communications, and the red shows that it does not score as well as other countries with similar economies. The United States does not score as well as other wealthy countries in any category, and Mexico falls behind not only the United States and Canada but also behind its economic equals in two categories. Clearly, there is room for all three countries to improve.

Access to Basic Knowledge

Education gives people the knowledge and skills they need to get better paying jobs in North America. All three countries have mandatory **primary education**. Mexico also requires one year of free preschool. (In the United States, this requirement varies, with some school systems, such as New York City, now offering universal preschool programs.) **Secondary education** is required through 12th grade in the United States, through 9th grade in Mexico, and until age 16 or 18 in Canada, depending on the province. Of the three countries, Canada scores the highest in Access to Basic Knowledge. Like the United States, Canada has an **adult literacy rate** of 99 percent compared to about 95 percent in Mexico. The United States is relatively weak in its overall score for Access to Basic Knowledge and also scores lower in junior high and high school enrollment than other wealthy countries.

Mexico scores higher than both Canada and the United States in lower secondary school (junior high) enrollment but falls behind on upper secondary school (high school) enrollment, with only 62 percent of eligible teens enrolled. Only about 37 percent of people ages 25 to 64 in Mexico have completed high school compared to 89 percent in Canada and the United States.

In Mexico a 40 percent poverty rate and a minimum wage of only 70 pesos a day (less than $5) means that many teens must go to work after 9th grade to help feed their families. Poor parents can't pay the fees or buy the uniforms, books, and supplies required for public high school. Most high schools are located in cities, so students in rural areas have even higher costs.

Access to Information and Communications

People need information they can trust so they can make good decisions and stay safe. The SPI scores in this category have to do with whether people are free to access all kinds of information and ideas.

	CANADA		UNITED STATES		MEXICO	
	Score	Rank	Score	Rank	Score	Rank
Mobile (cell) telephone subscriptions	78.4	101st	95.5	87th	85.8	98th
Internet users (per 100 people)	85.8	11th	84.2	13th	43.5	68th
Press Freedom Index	10.99	15th	23.49	36th	45.04	115th
Overall Access Info/Communication	84.56	25th	85.00	23rd	62.30	91st

Cell phones and Internet access have become important tools for getting information. Canada, the United States, and Mexico have a high number of cell telephone subscribers, but all score lower than other countries with similar economies. North America also has a high number of Internet users, and each country's numbers compare well to other countries with similar economies.

As part of the Access to Information and Communication score, the Social Progress Imperative used the Press Freedom Index. (In journalism, the word *press* means the news media companies and those who work for them.) The index is created each year by Reporters Without Borders (rsf.org), a nonprofit,

Organization of American States assistant secretary general Nestor Mendez delivers a speech during the inauguration of the forum Education in the Digital Era organized and held in Mexico City to focus on the introduction of information technologies and the use of virtual teaching systems.

nongovernmental organization that promotes freedom of information and freedom of the press. Index scores are based on four main categories:

- **Fairness of the news media (print, broadcast, and online):** *Are both sides of a story told? Are all cultural and political groups treated fairly in the news?*
- **Independence of news media:** *Are most of the news outlets owned by the government or by just a few companies that control what people hear?*
- **Level of respect for the safety/freedom of journalists:** *Do reporters face violence or jail for doing their jobs?*
- **Working environment for the news media:** *Do the laws protect journalists? Are the media afraid of the government? Organized crime? Terrorists?*

While Canada earned a high rank of 15th in the Press Freedom Index, the United States ranked 36th and Mexico ranked 115th. The United States earned a lower score than other wealthy countries in part because of its restrictions on sharing information that started after the terrorist attacks in September 2001. After the attacks, Congress passed laws that restricted access to information for reasons of national security. Many people were frightened by the attacks, so they supported the new policies. Others thought that citizens should always know what their government is doing.

Mexico is the deadliest country for journalists in the entire Western Hemisphere. Those who report about elections, demonstrations, drug cartels, or corrupt officials have suffered physical attacks, kidnappings, jail, and death. Between 2000 and July 2015, 86 journalists and media workers were murdered in Mexico just for doing their jobs.

Reporters, editors, camera operators, and photographers call for an end to violence against journalists in Mexico.

Health and Wellness

Every country has its own system of health care. All systems have the same goal, which is to provide health care for all their citizens and protect them from financial ruin from high medical bills. The SPI scores shown below can't be fully understood without knowing about the three very different health care systems in Canada, the United States, and Mexico.

	CANADA		UNITED STATES		MEXICO	
	Score	Rank	Score	Rank	Score	Rank
Life expectancy	81.2	13th	78.7	30th	77.1	34th
Outdoor air pollution attributable deaths	21.5	55th	33.6	78th	18.1	47th
Premature deaths	10.7	11th	14.3	35th	15.7	40th
Suicide rate	10.9	84th	10.75	81st	4.48	35th
Obesity rate	24.3	102nd	31.8	126th	32.8	127th
Overall Health and Wellness	76.09	17th	68.66	68th	72.02	45th

Canada has what is called a **universal health care** system. This means that every citizen of Canada has health insurance under the same system. The insurance is paid for by the public through taxes. Care is provided by private doctors and hospitals. Any Canadian can go to a hospital or see a doctor for free. With an overall rank of 17th, it's clear that the Canadian system works well. What's more, it costs less than the system in the lower-ranked United States ($5,718 per person in Canada compared to $9,145 in the United States in 2013).

In Canada everyone can see a doctor whenever needed.

As of 2016 the United States was still the only developed country in the world without universal health care. Instead, it has a mix of public and private health insurance options. Most people get insurance through their employer, who often pays at least part of the cost. The United States has a public system for senior citizens and the poor and another system for uninsured children. Military veterans have their own program.

The recent Affordable Care Act (ACA) passed in the United States requires every person to have health insurance. Thanks to the ACA, sick people are no longer denied insurance, and poor people can get help to pay part of the cost. Most insurance pays for routine checkups and for all or most of the cost of doctor visits, hospital care, and prescriptions. It's likely that the ranking of the United States will improve as more and more people have health insurance.

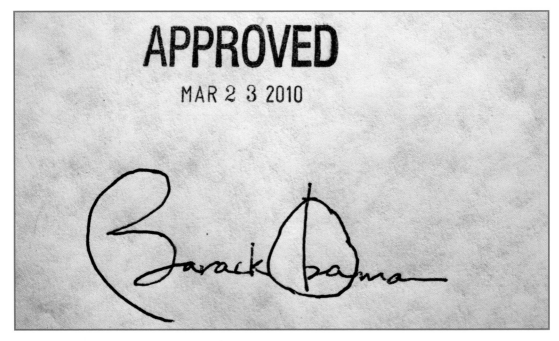

US President Barack Obama signed the Affordable Care Act on March 23, 2010, making affordable health insurance available to every American.

Mexico has two public health insurance options. Its IMSS program is available to people with jobs. It covers a range of medical care at low or no cost at IMSS hospitals and clinics. With help from the World Bank, Mexico added the

Seguro Popular program in 2003 to help the tens of millions of poor, uninsured people. While it doesn't cover everything, the popular insurance program covers 250 common procedures at general hospitals that serve the poor. The two programs are not coordinated with each other or with the system of high-quality, private care that serves the rich. The result is an inefficient system that does not treat all people equally.

Ecosystem Sustainability

If an activity is not sustainable, it means that there will come a time when you can no longer do it. For example, if you spend more money than you make, that activity is not sustainable because at some point you will run out of money. Ecosystem sustainability is when we care for resources like clean air, water, plants, and animals in such a way that they will still be here for future generations. To measure ecosystem sustainability, the Social Progress Imperative compared countries using three categories: greenhouse gas emissions, water use, and protection of biodiversity and habitat.

	CANADA		UNITED STATES		MEXICO	
	Score	Rank	Score	Rank	Score	Rank
Greenhouse gas emissions	516.41	4th	421.67	4th	371.87	4th
Water withdrawals as % of resources	1	54th	3	85th	4	110th
Biodiversity and habitat	58.40	77th	63.35	68th	62.32	72nd
Overall Ecosystem Sustainability	58.04	48th	51.63	74th	48.50	90th

Greenhouse gas emissions

Gases that trap heat in the earth's atmosphere are called greenhouse gases. Some of these gases are found naturally in the environment; others are released by the activities of humans. Carbon dioxide is the main greenhouse gas. It's released when we burn coal, natural gas, or oil. Plants absorb carbon dioxide so when we cut forests or clear land for houses, it puts even more carbon dioxide into the atmosphere.

Measuring **greenhouse gas emissions** is important because they have been linked to global warming and changes in world climate. Global warming is expected to have an unwanted effect on the environment by increasing the average temperature of the earth, changing where and how much it rains and snows, reducing the amount of ice and snow coverage, raising sea level, and increasing ocean acidity. On a scale of 1 (best) to 4 (worst), Canada, the United States, and Mexico all scored 4 because of high greenhouse emissions.

Water withdrawals as a percentage of resources

The water we drink and use to grow food, raise animals, and make electricity often comes from surface water (streams, rivers, and lakes). As long as the amount of precipitation (rain and snow) stays the same, the same amount of surface water is available each year. We also drill wells to get to water that is stored naturally underground. This **groundwater** is the source of drinking water for millions of North Americans. Unlike surface water, groundwater is not replaced every year. It can take hundreds or even thousands of years to replace the water that has been pumped out of the ground.

Using too much groundwater can create sinkholes.

The scores for sustainable water usage are based on how much water a country uses compared to how much is available. Canada's score of 1 means that it's placing low stress on its water supplies, but its world rank of 54th shows that there is room for improvement in how it manages its water resources.

The United States and Mexico have hundreds of thousands of acres of desert and semi-arid land that have little or unpredictable amounts of water. The US score of 3 shows medium-high stress on water resources, and Mexico's score of 4 means that its water resources are under extremely high stress.

Climate change will likely put more strain on water resources in North America. Analysts predict droughts—perhaps the worst in 1,000 years—for the Central Plains and southwestern United States and for northern Mexico. The worst drought on record in California has increased the use of limited groundwater as people try to keep California streams alive with fish and crops growing in the fields. When there isn't enough water to go around, people must make decisions about where the limited water should go. To lawns and swimming pools? To a $20 billion agriculture business? To industries like bottled water? To save fish? To generate electricity? In California people cannot agree on the answers to these questions, so they are being answered in court. With global warming and climate change, these are hard choices that all communities may soon face.

A volunteer delivers bottled water to a resident of Flint, Michigan, during a water crisis. The city's drinking water was found to be contaminated with lead after the government switched the supply to the polluted Flint River in an effort to save money.

Biodiversity and habitat

Biodiversity is the variety of plant and animal life in an area. Habitat is the environment in which a plant or animal lives. SPI scores rate the protection of land and ocean areas and consider the number of threatened or endangered plants and animals on a scale from 0 (no protection) to 100 (high protection).

Tiger salamanders are endangered because of destruction of their breeding pond habitats and as a result of being used as live bait for fishing.

In this category, Canada scores below both Mexico and the United States, putting its world rank at 77th. Canada has many resource conservation issues, including

- Overharvesting of fish and timber
- Water pollution from fish farms and agriculture
- Habitat destruction of the prairie ecosystem by farming
- High greenhouse gas emissions

The military macaw is one of more than 1,000 bird species found in Mexico.

The United States and Mexico are two of the most biodiverse countries in the world. US climates range from subarctic in Alaska to tropical in Hawaii. Mexico is home to 10 to 12 percent of all plants and animal species on earth, more than any other country in the Americas except Brazil and Colombia.

The United States ranked a low 68th in the protection of biodiversity and habitat; Mexico ranked 72nd. Both countries were named in the list of the Top 10 Countries Killing the Planet from a 2010 study by the University of Adelaide's Environment Institute in Australia in collaboration with the National University of Singapore and Princeton University in the United States. The United States was listed for its excessive use of fertilizers, high greenhouse gas emissions, water pollution, unsustainable fish harvesting, and the number of threatened plants and animals. Mexico also made the list because of the number of threatened plants and animals and for heavy **deforestation**, which is a likely cause of loss of habitat.

Deforestation in the state of Hidalgo, Mexico, can have impacts on thousands of communities.

Text-Dependent Questions

1. List two reasons why teens from poor families don't finish high school.
2. List two reasons that Canada scored below both the United States and Mexico in protecting biodiversity and habitat.
3. Which North American country scores lower than other countries with similar wealth in providing the Foundations of Well-being?
4. Why is it important to measure greenhouse gas emissions?
5. How does universal health care help the poor?

Research Project

Learn how climate change will affect US agriculture by taking a *Climate Change Expedition* and exploring the information on the US Environmental Protection Agency's website.

1. Go to epa.gov/climatechange/students/expeditions/agriculture/index.html.
2. Watch the video and follow the instructions on the screen.
3. When you complete your expedition, you can click the link to take another Climate Change Expedition in a different part of the world, or go to Step 4.
4. Click on the *Think Like a Scientist* tab at the top of the page. From the dropdown menu, select *You Can Be a Scientist Too!* Choose a project

that interests you or your class. Click on the link and find out how you can participate. (Note: The correct link for the budburst project is budburst.org/.) Ready for more? Go on to Step 5.

5. Click on the *Be Part of the Solution* tab at the top of the page. From the dropdown menu, select the *What You Can Do* link. Learn what you can do to help slow climate change. Report back to your class. Ready for more? Go on to Step 6.

6. Click again on the *Be Part of the Solution* tab at the top of the page. From the dropdown menu, select *Preparing for the Future.* Learn how people are preparing for climate change. Report back to your class.

Tens of thousands march
Mexico City to demand justi
over the fate of people w
have "disappeared" duri
the country's long-runni
drug w

CHAPTER 3

OPPORTUNITY

Words to Understand

Corruption: the dishonest behavior by people in positions of power for their own benefit.

Indigenous people: culturally distinct groups with long-standing ties to the land in a specific area. Indigenous groups in North America are descendants of the people the Europeans first met when they arrived.

Prejudice: an opinion that isn't based on facts or reason.

Stereotype: a common belief about the nature of the members of a specific group that is based on limited experience or incorrect information.

Transparency: means that the government operates in a way that is visible to and understood.

To reach our potential, we need personal freedom and opportunity. We want the freedom to move around, practice our religions, and make our own choices. We want an equal opportunity to get a college degree and have a voice in the political process. To understand how the level of opportunity differs from one country to another, the Social Progress Imperative scored 133 countries in the following categories:

- **Tolerance and Inclusion:** *Does everyone have the same opportunity to contribute?*
- **Personal Freedom and Choice:** *Are people allowed to make their own decisions?*

- **Personal Rights:** *Are people's individual rights restricted by the government?*
- **Access to Advanced Education:** *Does everyone have the opportunity to go to college?*

The table below shows the SPI scores and rankings for the three North American countries.

	CANADA		UNITED STATES		MEXICO	
	Score	Rank	Score	Rank	Score	Rank
GDP per capita	$41,894	14th	$51,340	6th	$16,291	51st
Tolerance and inclusion	84.88	3rd	74.46	15th	54.10	59th
Personal freedom and choice	88.41	9th	82.64	15th	63.08	59th
Personal rights	87.91	11th	82.16	24th	71.76	38th
Access to advanced education	85.11	3rd	89.47	1st	54.57	44th
Overall Opportunity	86.58	1st	82.18	8th	60.88	40th

Source: Social Progress Index

Both Canada and the United States are relatively strong in Access to Advanced Education. The United States score shows room for improvement in the category of Personal Rights.

Tolerance and Inclusion

Scores for Tolerance and Inclusion reflect the **prejudices** in a society that make it hard for some to succeed. Prejudices and **stereotypes** can result in unfair treatment that denies certain groups equal opportunities for housing, education, and jobs.

Tolerance for religion, immigrants, and homosexuals

Canada's relative strength in Tolerance and Inclusion is partly due to high scores for Religious Tolerance and for Tolerance for Immigrants, which was also a relative strength. Canada had the highest score of the three countries in the Tolerance for Homosexuals category. The US rank of 15th in this category will likely improve with the 2015 decision by the US Supreme Court that the right to same-sex marriage is protected by the US Constitution. Mexico's rank of 24th in Tolerance for Homosexuals shows room for improvement, but it's still a relative strength when compared with its economic equals.

Gay marriage was legalized in Canada in 2005, 10 years before it was made legal in the United States. As of 2016, gay marriage was legal in only some parts of Mexico.

The United States ranked 36th in Religious Tolerance and 11th in Tolerance for Immigrants. Mexico showed relative weaknesses in both categories, ranking 68th in Tolerance for Immigrants and 80th in Religious Tolerance. More than 80 percent of the population in Mexico is Catholic. Protestants are a small but growing minority in Mexico that is not always well tolerated.

Black Lives Matter

Black Lives Matter is a US movement started in response to the 2012 fatal shooting of an unarmed 17-year-old black American, Trayvon Martin, by George Zimmerman, a white Hispanic neighborhood watch volunteer in Florida. Many believed the shooting was racially motivated and were upset by a jury's failure to convict Zimmerman of murder.

After the death of Trayvon Martin, Black Lives Matter became the motto to protest police brutality against black Americans.

In the summer of 2014, another unarmed black teenager, Michael Brown, was shot and killed in Ferguson, Missouri, by a white police officer. Protests and riots broke out in Ferguson and other cities after a grand jury did not file criminal charges against the officer. The following spring, thousands more protesters took to the streets of Baltimore, Maryland, after the death of another black citizen, Freddie Gray, who died from injuries he got after he was arrested. The Baltimore protests turned violent and destructive, causing the governor to call in National Guard soldiers to take control of the streets. Officers in the case were charged with homicide.

The Black Lives Matter movement wants society to address what it calls the "systemic pattern of anti-black law enforcement in the United States." It promotes the idea that less money should be spent on police and jails and more on jobs, housing, and schools in poverty-stricken majority black communities.

Discrimination and violence against minorities

North America has a history marked with discrimination and violence against **indigenous people** and people of African descent. SPI ranks in this category are Canada 8th, United States 31st, and Mexico 61st.

Community safety net

If you were in trouble, do you have relatives or friends you can count on to help you whenever you need them? In Canada, 94 percent of people who were asked this question said, yes, they had friends and family they can count on. In the United States 90 percent said yes. Mexico showed a relative weakness in this category, with only 77 percent.

Personal Freedom and Choice

The scores in the category of Personal Freedom and Choice help us understand how much freedom people have to make decisions about their lives, religions, marriage, and contraception. It also considers the level of corruption in a country because corruption has the power to limit everyone's freedom.

Freedom of religion

The SPI scores show Canada with a high level of religious freedom (score 4 of 4) and both the United States and Mexico with moderate levels (score 3 of 4). The constitutions of all three countries guarantee religious freedom, and people are to be protected by law if their religious freedom is violated.

Early marriage and contraception

Teen marriage makes it hard for young people to take advantage of the opportunities that are available to them. Young people who marry before they finish high school often drop out to go to work. Canada, the United States, and Mexico were all relatively weak in this category, all scoring lower than other countries with similar economies.

Early marriage in North America often follows pregnancy. Child care is expensive, so young mothers may quit school to stay home with the baby while the young father goes to work to support the family. Divorce or abandonment in any country can leave mothers of all ages in poverty. More and more women use contraception (birth control) to limit the number of children they have. The percentages of women who are married or in a long-term relationship who use modern methods of family planning are 87 percent in Canada, 85 percent in the United States, and 81 percent in Mexico.

Freedom over life choices

Are you satisfied with your freedom to choose what you do with your life? When asked this question, the majority of people in Canada (91 percent), the United States (87 percent), and Mexico (76 percent) said that they were satisfied. While those numbers may seem high, they represent relative weaknesses for the United States and Mexico.

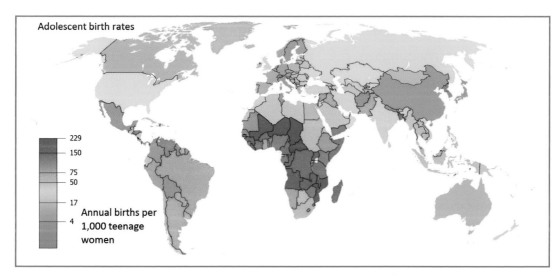

Teen pregnancy rates around the world.

Corruption

Corruption creates an unfair society that favors some people over others. When those in power take advantage of their positions for their own benefit, we say that they are corrupt or that there is corruption in the system. Corruption often takes the form of accepting bribes to break the rules or just to do the job they were hired to do. Of the North American countries, Canada's government (ranks 8th) has the most **transparency**. The United States has a high rank of 15th, but Mexico ranks 82nd with a score that is half that of the United States.

Countries with a high poverty rate like Mexico have more corruption, but it's not just poor countries that have it. In the United States, rich individuals and ultra-rich corporations have been allowed to put unlimited amounts of money into political campaigns in recent years. Many people think that the influence of big money in Washington, D.C., is a form of corruption because it creates a government where only the rich are represented.

Citizens protest the billions of dollars spent by big business and wealthy individuals to influence the outcome of US elections.

Personal Rights

In 1948 the General Assembly of the United Nations accepted the Universal Declaration of Human Rights, in which it recognized that "the inherent dignity and ... the equal and inalienable rights of all members of the human family is the foundation of freedom, justice and peace in the world." Canada, the United States, and Mexico all voted in favor of the declaration. When laws or policies exist to restrict human rights or when police and courts fail to enforce the laws, people's opportunities become limited.

Freedom of movement

People should be able to move around inside their country and travel to other countries and return. Fortunately, the countries of North America agree. Canada and Mexico earned top scores in this category, meaning that people are free to move around the country and to leave and return. The United States scored lower at least partly because of travel restrictions and a complex security screening system at airports that started after the terrorist attacks involving airplanes in 2001. The US Transportation Security Agency x-rays luggage, scans passengers, and performs random searches at airports and maintains a "no fly" list of names to help keep suspected terrorists from boarding airplanes.

Freedom of assembly/association and freedom of speech

Freedom to gather peacefully and to associate freely with organizations such as political parties and trade unions is guaranteed in the constitutions of Canada, the United States, and Mexico. Freedom of speech is also guaranteed in all three countries. Unfortunately, freedoms guaranteed by law are sometimes restricted in actual practice.

Mass Incarceration = Mass Discrimination in the United States

In the United States, blacks and Hispanics are incarcerated (jailed) at higher rates and serve longer sentences than do whites. One of every 15 black males over 18 years old is in prison, and 1 of every 3 black men will spend time in prison during his lifetime.

Race/Ethnicity	% of US Population	% of US Incarcerated	Incarceration Rate (per 100,000)
White (non-Hispanic)	64	39	450
Hispanic	16	19	831
Black	13	40	2,306

Source: US Census Data, 2010

The United States has 5 percent of the world's population and a shocking 25 percent of the world's prison population. The US prison system is privatized, which means that it's run by private companies for profit, not by the government. The cost to US taxpayers is estimated at around $80 billion per year. Prison reform advocates have called for a 50 percent reduction in the number of people in jail, starting with the release of nonviolent offenders.

Canada and Mexico have few restrictions and are among the highest-ranked countries in the world in the category of Freedom of Assembly/Association. More restrictions in the United States earned it a lower score and its rank of 48th, a relative weakness when compared to other wealthy countries.

In 2011 a group called Occupy Wall Street organized protests in New York City's Wall Street financial district against unfair control and mismanagement of the world's financial resources by the richest 1 percent of the population.

The Occupy movement spread to dozens of cities around the world. There were many clashes with police, who used tear gas, pepper spray, flash grenades, and rubber bullets to disperse protesters. Many protesters were injured; many were jailed.

In the category of Freedom of Speech, the United States has a high ranking (1st), which is a relative strength when compared to other wealthy countries. Canada and Mexico share the rank of 15th.

The Occupy Wall Street movement was picked up in Canada and Mexico.

Whistleblowers: The Wikileaks Effect

A whistleblower is someone who reveals the illegal, dangerous, or unethical activity of an individual or organization to the public or to the people in charge. In 2006 Julian Assange created the WikiLeaks.com website to allow whistleblowers to share information without revealing their identity. In the years that followed, WikiLeaks published thousands of secret US government documents. Much of the information published was provided by two whistleblowers whose identities were later discovered.

Chelsea Manning was a US Army soldier and intelligence analyst. She released secret documents to shed light on underreported civilian casualties in the Iraq war and the torture of suspected terrorists in military prison. Manning also shared hundreds of thousands of secret cables between the US State Department and its embassies around the world. The cables revealed US spying on other countries and embarrassing misconduct by the US and some of its allies. Manning was arrested in 2010. She pleaded guilty to charges of espionage and was sentenced to 35 years in jail. In 2014 she was awarded the Sam Adams Award for her whistleblower activities. The award is given by the Sam Adams Associates for Integrity in Intelligence, a group of retired CIA officers.

Former CIA employee Edward Snowden worked for a contractor for the US National Security Agency. He gave WikiLeaks proof of widespread government spying on private citizens. Snowden was charged with crimes that carry combined sentences of up to 30 years in prison. He left the United States in 2013 to avoid prosecution, eventually receiving permission from Russia to live there. He was awarded the MacBride Peace Prize in 2013 and the Sam Adams Award, the Right Livelihood Award, and the Stuttgart Peace Prize in 2014.

WikiLeaks creator Julian Assange was given diplomatic asylum at the Ecuadorian embassy in London in 2012. If he leaves the embassy, Assange will be immediately arrested and sent to Sweden for questioning by Swedish police on an unrelated matter. Once in Sweden, he fears that he will be forced to go to the United States where he would face an investigation into his role in

WikiLeaks and possible charges of espionage. In January 2016, the Working Group on Arbitrary Detention (WGAD) of the United Nations Human Rights Council found that the refusals of the UK and Sweden to let Assange leave the Ecuadorian embassy without being arrested is an arbitrary and illegal detention. WGAD requested that Assange be granted his freedom and ruled that he should be able to ask for compensation (payment) from the UK and Sweden for their actions. WGAD's decision is considered a victory not only for Assange but for all whistleblowers. Assange received the Sam Adams Award and was named Readers' Choice for *Time* magazine's Person of the Year in 2010.

Protesters showing support for Julian Assange protest outside the Ecuadorian embassy in London.

Many view Assange and the whistleblowers as heroes and believe that WikiLeaks.com is an important tool for letting the public learn of misconduct by governments around the world. WikiLeaks defends its right to publish with Article 19 of the United Nations' Universal Declaration of Human Rights, which says:

Everyone has the right to freedom of opinion and expression; this right includes freedom to hold opinions without interference and to seek, receive, and impart information and ideas through any media and regardless of frontiers.

Political rights

For those who enjoy the rights of citizenship and participation in the political process, it may be hard to imagine that some people in the world have no political rights. They cannot vote or hold public office. They have no say in what their government does, and they have no right to complain. Fortunately, the situation in North America couldn't be more different. Canada and the United States have full political rights, both scoring 1 (full rights) on a 7-point (no rights) scale. Mexico scored a 3 for a rank of 60th, which is about the same as other countries with similar wealth.

Private property rights

Private property rights are generally protected in Canada, the United States, and Mexico, but governments usually reserve the right to take property under some circumstances. In most cases, the owner is paid for the property at a fair market price, as in the following examples:

- Property is needed as a place to put utilities, parks, schools, etc.
- Property is needed to protect the environment or because it's a hazard.
- Property needs to be protected for its historical or cultural value.

In a process called civil forfeiture, police can take property that they think was used in a crime or resulted from criminal activity. Civil forfeiture laws were originally created to help shut down large criminal organizations by taking the resources that kept them in business. Critics say that police in the United States and Canada are using these laws against people to take cash, cars, and even houses for profit instead of to fight crime. There is a large public outcry against this behavior in both countries, and progress has been made. New Mexico recently became the second US state to ban civil forfeiture until the person is convicted of a crime in court.

With a rank of 3rd, Canada has a high score in the category of Property Rights. The United States ranks 17th, which is a relative weakness compared to the other high GDP per capita countries. Mexico ranks 39th, which is about the same as the scores of its economic equals.

Access to Advanced Education

North American countries show several relative strengths in the category of Access to Advanced Education, as shown with the blue numbers in the following chart of SPI scores and ranks.

	CANADA		UNITED STATES		MEXICO	
	Score	Rank	Score	Rank	Score	Rank
Women's average years in school	15.0	1st	13.9	4th	10.1	71st
Loss of education due to inequality	0.04	21st	0.07	38th	0.21	70th
Globally ranked universities	26	3rd	181	1st	13	3rd
Years of tertiary education (after grade 12)	1.51	3rd	1.76	1st	0.62	41st
Overall Access to Advanced Education	85.11	3rd	89.47	1st	54.57	44th

Canada is relatively strong in the number of years of school that women complete when compared to other countries with very high social progress. Both Canada and the United States show strengths in tertiary education (education after high school).

The United States and Mexico are strong in the number of globally ranked universities in their countries. One relative weakness was revealed for the United States in the estimated loss of education that people experience due to social and economic inequality in the country. Even though it scored higher than Mexico, the US score is not as high as the scores of most other countries with other wealthy economies.

More education is linked to higher pay and lower unemployment for people in every developed country. The following chart shows how education pays off for workers in the United States.

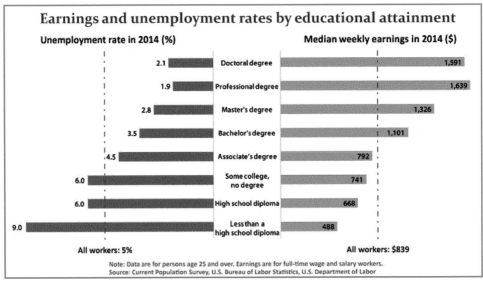

Source: US Department of Labor

Text-Dependent Questions

1. Name two legal reasons that allow the government to take personal property from its owner.
2. Do you think that Chelsea Manning is a traitor or a hero? Why?
3. How does early marriage interfere with getting a secondary education?
4. Which two North American countries have the most globally ranked universities?

Research Project

1. The Prison Policy Initiative (prisonpolicy.org) was founded in 2001 to publicize how mass incarceration (imprisonment) in the United States hurts our society. Follow the instructions below and use the links to go to the Prison Policy Initiative's website to answer questions about mass incarceration.

   Are whites, blacks, Hispanics, and Native Americans a bigger or smaller percentage of the prison population than they should be in your state?

   • Go to prisonpolicy.org/profiles/
   • Select your state, or a state you are interested in, from the interactive map.
   • Look at the graphs about the rates of incarceration.
   • Which race/ethnic group is most overrepresented in prison in your state? Which is the most underrepresented?

- Look at other states. How do those numbers compare with your state?

Answer the questions below by following the link provided after the question.

- Which countries incarcerate the most people per 100,000 population? prisonpolicy.org/atlas/globalincarc2004.html
- Some countries have low incarceration rates of fewer than 150 people a year per 100,000 population. Are there more countries with low rates or more countries with higher rates? prisonpolicy.org/atlas/globalprisonrateunder150.html
- Which three countries have the most people in jail? prisonpolicy.org/atlas/globalprisonersnumber.html
- What percent of the world's prisoners are in those three countries? prisonpolicy.org/atlas/globalprisonerspercentage.html

2. Use the interactive map at the Migration Policy Institute (migrationpolicy.org) website and follow the instructions to complete the table below showing how many North American immigrants are in each country.

🇨🇦	Canadians in Mexico	9,000
🇲🇽	Mexicans in Canada	
🇺🇸	Americans in Canada	
🇺🇸	Americans in Mexico	
🇨🇦	Canadians in United States	
🇲🇽	Mexicans in United States	

a. Go to migrationpolicy.org/programs/data-hub/charts/international-migrant-population-country-origin-and-destination

b. Beneath the world map, select **Mexico** as the country and **Migrants in country** as your display options.

c. A green diamond appears over Mexico on the map.

d. Point to the orange circle over Canada to display the number of migrants in Mexico from Canada. The number is 9,000, which is already written on the chart.

e. Next, point to the orange circle over the United States. Record the number of migrants in Mexico from the United States in the chart.

f. Change the selected country to the United States. Point to the orange circles above Canada and Mexico. Record the number of migrants from each country in the chart.

g. Change the selected country to Canada. Use the same process you used above to find and record the number of migrants from Mexico and the United States in Canada in the chart.

NORTH AMERICAN COUNTRIES AT A GLANCE

Regional Overview

North America contains 13 percent of the world's land and is home to 6 percent of the world's people. There are only three countries in North American: Canada, the United States, and Mexico. Even with different governments, religions, and languages, these countries have cultural and economic ties. They share a history of European colonization from which each declared its independence (Canada in 1867 and the United States in 1775 from England, and Mexico in 1810 from Spain).

Tourism between the countries is common, and tens of thousands of Americans and Canadians live in Mexico during the winter. Millions of Mexicans live and work in the United States. Canada and the United States sell more of their exports to each other than to any other countries. The United States is Mexico's main market for exports; Canada is the third largest. Mexico is number three on the list of countries that buy the most from Canada and the United States. Here are some quick facts to help you get to know the countries of North America.

CANADA

QUICK STATS

Population: 35,099,836
Urban Population: 81.8%
Comparative Size: second-largest country; slightly larger than the US
Gross Domestic Product (per capita): $44,800 (29th highest)
Gross Domestic Product (by sector): agriculture 1.7%, industry 28.2%, services 70.1%
Government: a parliamentary democracy, a federation, and a constitutional monarchy
Languages: English (official) 58.7%, French (official) 22%, Punjabi 1.4%, Italian 1.3%, Spanish 1.3%, German 1.3%, Cantonese 1.2%, Tagalog 1.2%, Arabic 1.1%, other 10.5%

SOCIAL PROGRESS SNAPSHOT

Social Progress Index: 86.89 (+25.89 above 61.00 world average)
Basic Human Needs: 94.89 (+26.56 above 68.33 world average)
Foundations of Well-being: 79.22 (+12.77 above/below 66.45 world average)
Opportunity: 86.58 (+38.35 above 48.23 world average)

A land of vast distances and rich natural resources, Canada became a self-governing dominion in 1867, while retaining ties to the British crown. Economically and technologically, the nation has developed in parallel with the United States, its neighbor to the south across the world's longest unfortified border. Canada faces the political challenges of meeting public demands for quality improvements in health care, education, social services, and economic competitiveness, as well as responding to the particular concerns of predominantly francophone Quebec. Canada also aims to develop its diverse energy resources while maintaining its commitment to the environment.

MEXICO

QUICK STATS

Population: 121,736,809
Urban Population: 79.2%
Comparative Size: 14th largest; slightly less than three times the size of Texas
Gross Domestic Product (per capita): $17,900 (92nd highest)
Gross Domestic Pproduct (by sector): agriculture 3.5%, industry 36.4%, services 60.1%
Government: federal republic
Languages: Spanish only 92.7%, Spanish and indigenous languages (Mayan and Nahuatl and regional languages) 5.7%, indigenous only 0.8%, unspecified 0.8%

SOCIAL PROGRESS SNAPSHOT

Social Progress Index: 67.50 (+6.50 above 61.00 world average)
Basic Human Needs: 72.81 (+4.48 above 68.33 world average)
Foundations of Well-being: 68.82 (+2.37 above 66.45 world average)
Opportunity: 60.88 (+12.65 above 48.23 world average)

The site of several advanced Amerindian civilizations—including the Olmec, Toltec, Teotihuacan, Zapotec, Maya, and Aztec—Mexico was conquered and colonized by Spain in the early 16th century. Administered as the Viceroyalty of New Spain for three centuries, it achieved independence early in the 19th century. Economic and social concerns include low wages, high underemployment, inequitable income distribution, and few advancement opportunities for the largely indigenous population in the impoverished southern states. Since 2007, Mexico's powerful drug-trafficking organizations have engaged in bloody feuding, resulting in tens of thousands of drug-related homicides.

UNITED STATES

QUICK STATS

Population: 321,368,864
Urban Population: 81.6%
Comparative Size: third-largest country in the world; about half the size of Russia; about three-tenths the size of Africa; about half the size of South America (or slightly larger than Brazil); slightly larger than China; more than twice the size of the European Union
Gross Domestic Product (per capita): $54,600 (19th highest)
Gross Domestic Product (by sector): agriculture 1.6%, industry 20.7%, services 77.7%
Government: constitution-based federal republic; strong democratic tradition
Languages: English 79.2%, Spanish 12.9%, other Indo-European 3.8%, Asian and Pacific island 3.3%, other 0.9% (Note: Data represent the languages spoken at home. The United States has no official language, but English has official status in 31 of the 50 states; Hawaiian is an official language in the state of Hawaii.)

SOCIAL PROGRESS SNAPSHOT

Social Progress Index: 82.85 (+21.85 above 61.00 world average)
Basic Human Needs: 91.23 (+22.90 above 68.33 world average)
Foundations of Well-being: 75.15 (+8.70 above 66.45 world average)
Opportunity: 82.18 (+33.95 above 48.23 world average)

Britain's American colonies broke with the mother country in 1776 and were recognized as the new nation of the United States of America following the Treaty of Paris in 1783. During the 19th and 20th centuries, 37 new states were added to the original 13 as the nation expanded across the North American continent and acquired a number of overseas possessions. The United States is the world's most powerful nation state. Since the end of World War II, the economy has achieved relatively steady growth, low unemployment and inflation, and rapid advances in technology.

The Inuit were the original
inhabitants of what is now
known as Canada.

CONCLUSION

Measuring social progress is not an idle pastime. It's a necessity.

Great achievements in agriculture and medicine increased the world's population from around three billion in 1960 to six billion just 50 years later. There are more than seven billion people living on the planet today, and more than nine billion people will call earth home before 2050. Providing for basic human needs, making available the foundations of well-being, and creating opportunities for every person in a sustainable way is the biggest challenge ever faced by humankind.

Business as usual is no longer an option. It's clear that poverty and income inequality rob billions of people of even the most basic necessities of food, water, shelter, and medical care. We're seeing increasing local violence, terrorism, and war in places that have high poverty, little education, and no opportunity. It's become clear that we cannot continue to put more and more greenhouse gases into the atmosphere nor can we continue to use more water and other resources in a year than the world can replace. We have begun to suffer the extreme weather conditions that are the calling card of climate change.

Solutions to these problems will come from young people like you. Measuring and understanding social progress is a good place to start.

The less money a country has, the harder it is to make sure that the basic needs of all of its citizens are met. But even in rich countries like the United States and Canada many people still lack the basic necessities of life: clean water, sanitation, enough food, adequate shelter, basic medicine, and safety. The people most likely to be without the basics in any country are the poor, old, mentally and physically disabled, minorities, indigenous groups, and immigrants.

To achieve a high rate of well-being, societies must spend money on education, health, and environmental protection. People also need their rights and freedoms protected by the laws and in the courts and opportunities that allow them to improve their lives. We have seen that a high GDP does not always result in increased well-being. Canada, whose economy ranks 14th in the world, also ranks 14th in providing the Foundations of Well-being, but the United States ranks 6th in economy but only 35th in the Foundations of Well-being.

If the countries of North America were considered as a single country, a Social Progress Snapshot like those in Chapter 4 can be calculated by averaging their SPI scores. Using simple averages, North America's Snapshot might look like this:

SOCIAL PROGRESS SNAPSHOT FOR NORTH AMERICA
Social Progress Index: 79.08 (+14.69 above 64.39 world average)
Basic Human Needs: 86.31 (+15.49 above 70.82 world average)
Foundations of Well-being: 74.39 (+6.71 above 67.68 world average)
Opportunity: 76.54 (+24.51 above 52.03 world average)

Clearly, the average North American enjoys a higher level of social progress than does the average world citizen. Even so, there's always room for improvement. The Social Progress Index has shown us how economic and social inequalities can mean that even within the same country, millions of people can struggle while others enjoy lives of relative ease. As societies start to use social progress to measure success, social progress should increase and many people's lives will improve.

Series Glossary

Anemia: a condition in which the blood doesn't have enough healthy red blood cells, most often caused by not having enough iron

Aquifer: an underground layer of water-bearing permeable rock, from which groundwater can be extracted using a water well

Asylum: protection granted by a nation to someone who has left their native country as a political refugee

Basic human needs: the things people need to stay alive: clean water, sanitation, food, shelter, basic medical care, safety

Biodiversity: the variety of life that is absolutely essential to the health of different ecosystems

Carbon dioxide (CO_2): a greenhouse gas that contributes to global warming and climate change

Censorship: the practice of officially examining books, movies, and other media and art, and suppressing unacceptable parts

Child mortality rate: the number of children that die before their fifth birthday for every 1,000 babies born alive

Communicable diseases: medical conditions spread by airborne viruses or bacteria or through bodily fluids such as malaria, tuberculosis, and HIV/AIDS; also called **infectious diseases;** differ from **noncommunicable diseases**, medical conditions not caused by infection and requiring long-term treatment such as diabetes or heart disease

Contraception: any form of birth control used to prevent pregnancy

Corruption: the dishonest behavior by people in positions of power for their own benefit

Deforestation: the clearing of trees, transforming a forest into cleared land

Desalination: a process that removes minerals (including salt) from ocean water

Discrimination: the unjust or prejudicial treatment of different categories of people, especially on the grounds of race, age, or sex

Ecosystem: a biological community of interacting organisms and their physical environment

Ecosystem sustainability: when we care for resources like clean air, water, plants, and animals so that they will be available to future generations

Emissions: the production and discharge of something, especially gas or radiation

Ethnicities: social groups that have a common national or cultural tradition

Extremism: the holding of extreme political or religious views; fanaticism

Famine: a widespread scarcity of food that results in malnutrition and starvation on a large scale

Food desert: a neighborhood or community with no walking access to affordable, nutritious food

Food security: having enough to eat at all times

Greenhouse gas emissions: any of the atmospheric gases that contribute to the greenhouse effect by absorbing infrared radiation produced by solar warming of the earth's surface. They include carbon dioxide (CO_2), methane (CH_4), nitrous oxide (NO_2), and water vapor.

Gross domestic product (GDP): the total value of all products and services created in a country during a year

GDP per capita (per person): the gross domestic product divided by the number of people in the country. For example, if the GDP for a country is one hundred million dollars ($100,000,000) and the population is one million people (1,000,000), then the GDP per capita (value created per person) is $100.

Habitat: environment for a plant or animal, including climate, food, water, and shelter

Incarceration: the condition of being imprisoned

Income inequality: when the wealth of a country is spread very unevenly among the population

Indigenous people: culturally distinct groups with long-standing ties to the land in a specific area

Inflation: when the same amount money buys less from one day to the next. Just because things cost more does not mean that people have more money. Low-income people trapped in a high inflation economy can quickly find themselves unable to purchase even the basics like food.

Infrastructure: permanent features required for an economy to operate such as transportation routes and electric grids; also systems such as education and courts

Latrine: a communal outdoor toilet, such as a trench dug in the ground

Literate: able to read and write

Malnutrition: lack of proper nutrition, caused by not having enough to eat, not eating enough of the right things, or being unable to use the food that one does eat

Maternal mortality rate: the number of pregnant women who die for every 100,000 births.

Natural resources: industrial materials and assets provided by nature such as metal deposits, timber, and water

Nongovernmental organization (NGO): a nonprofit, voluntary citizens' group organized on a local, national, or international level. Examples include organizations that support human rights, advocate for political participation, and work for improved health care.

Parliament: a group of people who are responsible for making the laws in some kinds of government

Prejudice: an opinion that isn't based on facts or reason

Preventive care: health care that helps an individual avoid illness

Primary school: includes grades 1–6 (also known as elementary school); precedes **secondary** and **tertiary education**, schooling beyond the primary grades; secondary generally corresponds to high school, and tertiary generally means college-level

Privatization: the transfer of ownership, property, or business from the government to the private sector (the part of the national economy that is not under direct government control)

Sanitation: conditions relating to public health, especially the provision of clean drinking water and adequate sewage disposal

Stereotypes: are common beliefs about the nature of the members of a specific group that are based on limited experience or incorrect information

Subsistence agriculture: a system of farming that supplies the needs of the farm family without generating any surplus for sale

Surface water: the water found above ground in streams, lakes, and rivers

Tolerance: a fair, objective, and permissive attitude toward those whose opinions, beliefs, practices, racial or ethnic origins, and so on differ from one's own

Trafficking: dealing or trading in something illegal

Transparency: means that the government operates in a way that is visible to and understood by the public

Universal health care: a system in which every person in a country has access to doctors and hospitals

Urbanization: the process by which towns and cities are formed and become larger as more and more people begin living and working in central areas

Well-being: the feeling people have when they are healthy, comfortable, and happy

Whistleblower: someone who reveals private information about the illegal activities of a person or organization

Index

RESOURCES

Continue exploring the world of development through this assortment of online and print resources. Follow links, stay organized, and maintain a critical perspective. Also, seek out news sources from outside the country in which you live.

Websites

Social Progress Imperative: socialprogressimperative.org
United Nations—Human Development Indicators: hdr.undp.org/en/countries and Sustainable Development Goals: un.org/
      sustainabledevelopment/sustainable-development-goals
World Bank—World Development Indicators: data.worldbank.org/data-catalog/world-development-indicators
World Health Organization—country statistics: who.int/gho/countries/en
U.S. State Department—human rights tracking site: humanrights.gov/dyn/countries.html
Oxfam International: oxfam.org/en
Amnesty International: amnesty.org/en
Human Rights Watch: hrw.org
Reporters without Borders: en.rsf.org
CIA—The World Factbook: cia.gov/library/publications/the-world-factbook

Books

Literary and classics
The Good Earth, Pearl S. Buck
Grapes of Wrath, John Steinbeck
The Jungle, Upton Sinclair

Nonfiction—historical/classic
Angela's Ashes, Frank McCourt
Lakota Woman, Mary Crow Dog with Richard Erdoes
Orientalism, Edward Said
Silent Spring, Rachel Carson
The Souls of Black Folk, W.E.B. Du Bois

Nonfiction: development and policy—presenting a range of views
Behind the Beautiful Forevers: Life, Death, and Hope in a Mumbai Undercity, Katherine Boo
The Bottom Billion: Why the Poorest Countries Are Failing and What Can Be Done About It, Paul Collier
The End of Poverty, Jeffrey D. Sachs
For the Common Good: Redirecting the Economy toward Community, the Environment, and a Sustainable Future,
      Herman E. Daly
I Am Malala: The Girl Who Stood Up for Education and Was Shot by the Taliban, Malala Yousafzai and Christina Lamb
The Life You Can Save: Acting Now to End World Poverty, Peter Singer
Mismeasuring Our Lives: Why GDP Doesn't Add Up, Joseph E. Stiglitz, Amartya Sen, and Jean-Paul Fitoussi
Rachel and Her Children: Homeless Families in America, Jonathan Kozol
The White Man's Burden: Why the West's Efforts to Aid the Rest Have Done So Much Ill and So Little Good, William Easterly

Foreword writer Michael Green is an economist, author, and cofounder of the Social Progressive Imperative. A UK native and graduate of Oxford University, Green has worked in aid and development for the British government and taught economics at Warsaw University.

Author Judy Boyd has designed and developed self-study workbooks, instructor-led courses, and online learning modules to teach language, technology, and mapping. She holds a B.S. in cartography and an M.S. in interactive telecommunications. She lives in Santa Fe, New Mexico, where she works as a freelance writer and watercolor artist.